Overcome Being Poor or Homeless

Roland John Gilbert

Scripture quotations marked "NIV" are taken from THE HOLY BIBLE, NEW INTERNATIONAL VERSION. Copyright© 1973, 1978, 1984 International Bible Society. Used by permission of Zondervan Bible Publishers. All rights reserved.

Scripture quotations marked "NKJV™" are taken from the New King James Version®. Copyright© 1982 by Thomas Nelson, Inc. Used by permission. All rights reserved.

Scripture quotations marked (NLT) are taken from the Holy Bible, New Living Translation, Copyright© 1996, 2004, 2007. Used by permission of Tyndale House Publishers, Inc., Carol Stream, Illinois 60188. All rights reserved.

Noted Individuals Who Have Experienced Homelessness is taken from Celebrity Research Lists. Used by permission of Celebrity Research Lists. All rights reserved.

Attitude is taken from **Strengthening Your Grip on Attitudes**, by Chuck Swindoll, IFL Audio Sermon SYG7A. Used by permission of Chuck Swindoll and Insight for Living. All rights reserved.

Mom's Pride by Dennis McCarthy is taken from the Daily News of Los Angeles Copyright© 2007. Used by permission of the Daily News, Los Angeles, California. All rights reserved.

Copyright © 2011 by Roland J. Gilbert
First Edition

Without limiting the rights under copyright reserved above, no part of this publication may be reproduced, stored in or introduced into a retrieval system, or transmitted, in any form or by any means (electronic, mechanical, photocopying, recording, or otherwise), without the prior written permission of the copyright owner.

ISBN-10: 1466346825
ISBN-13: 978-1466346826

Printed in the United States of America.
ALL RIGHTS RESERVED WORLDWIDE.

BOOKS BY ROLAND J. GILBERT

The Ghetto Solution. Gilbert, Roland J., and Cheo Tyehimba-Taylor. Waco, Texas: WRS Publishing, 1993. ISBN: 1-56796-021-9.

Power Parenting for Poor People. Gilbert, Roland J. Los Angeles, California: CreateSpace/Amazon.com, 2013. ISBN-13: 978-1491261248. ISBN-10: 1491261242

Please visit facebook.com/OvercomeBeingPoor and twitter.com/overcomebeingpo for updates and news.

Please email Roland at
OvercomeBeingPoor@Yahoo.com

Please write to Roland at
P.O. Box 582, Burbank, CA 91503

Please call Roland at (213) 293-5643

DEDICATION

I dedicate this book to the poor in America, to the Philanthropy Industry, with $316 billion spent in 2012 and more than 9.4 million employed, and to the Social Services Industry spending billions of dollars annually throughout the United States and employing millions of people. It is time to learn, change, and grow because what you have been doing is not eliminating poverty—but making it an industry—because of your *Philanthropic Colonialism*.

We will never eliminate poverty and homelessness in America until we are willing to learn, change, and grow. The 3 major reasons we fail are:

1. We separate poverty from homelessness.

2. We do not see, nor understand, that poverty is a culture.

3. All of our Philanthropic and Social Services Models are based upon Rational Choice Theory and Cognitive Dissonance Theory—both of these theories do not include, nor recognize, that poverty is a culture.

Therefore, mental illness and case management has become the modern plantation for the poor and uneducated.

There is no shame in being born into poverty. The shame is that we have an American Poverty Industry built upon *Philanthropic Colonialism* that perpetuates multi-generational poverty.

Poor people and homeless people love my books and workshops so much because my books and workshops transport them from a Culture of Poverty into a Culture of Success.

—Roland J. Gilbert

ACKNOWLEDGMENTS

Thank you, Father, for choosing me and giving me your Holy Spirit, and for placing me in Christ Jesus for righteousness and eternal life with you.

I also thank Juanita L. Alvarez, Larry Lockett and Hector Beltran for your encouragement and valuable suggestions on my manuscript.

I give special thanks to my friend, Linda Perez, for dropping everything to pick up my manuscript and help me polish it to a bright shine.

"The reasonable man adapts himself to the world; the unreasonable one persists in trying to adapt the world to himself. Therefore all progress depends on the unreasonable man."

—George Bernard Shaw

CONTENTS

What Is Wrong with You?	1
Which Groups Are You In?	3
The Natural Success Cycle of Life	9
What Do You Need to Learn?	13
How Do You Need to Change?	17
Where Do You Need to Grow?	25
How to Get Better Results from Social Service Agencies	33
7 Daily Habits to Overcome Being Poor	39
Recommended Resources	41
Appendix A…Some Truths in This Book	43
Appendix B…Some People Who Overcame Being Poor and Homeless	45
Appendix C…Some Truths from Other People	61
Appendix D…An Example of True Love and Normal Parenting	67
Appendix E…The Charitable-Industrial Complex	73

WHAT IS WRONG WITH YOU?

> *"Train up a child in the way he should go,
> and when he is old he will not depart from it."*
> Proverbs 22:6
> The Holy Bible (NKJV™)

Imagine you must prepare a full dinner that you have never made before. Someone gives you the recipe. But what you don't know is that part of the recipe is missing, or maybe some of the instructions are incorrect. But you don't know any of this because you are new to cooking. How well will you make the dinner? Is it your fault? Should you have known better?

Imagine having only part of the instructions to repair your car, or some of the instructions being incorrect. But you don't know it because you are new to auto repair. What kind of job would you do? Is it your fault? Should you have known better?

In your childhood, and while growing up, you were sometimes given incomplete and incorrect instructions on how to be successful in life. But you didn't know it because you were new to life then, and what you learned became habitual ways of thinking, feeling, and acting. What kind of life have you been making? Is it your fault? Should you have known better?

There is nothing wrong with you. The problem is the experiences and information you did, or did not, receive while growing up. It is not your fault, but it is your responsibility (ability to respond) to do something about it—if you choose to.

This book gives you correct instructions to be more successful in life—every part of your life. It is up to you to:

1. Choose to receive it and;
2. Choose to use it.

Knowledge is *not* power. The application of knowledge is power! Only the knowledge you choose to use and practice every day will give you power.

Dorothy Law Nolte, Ph.D., family counselor and author of the world famous parenting poem, "Children Learn What They Live," summarizes, in Appendix C, how what happens to us as children affects us as adults. You are facing tremendous obstacles that will take dedication, hard work, and help to overcome.

Dr. Karl Menninger, MD, psychiatrist, and founder of the world renowned Menninger Psychiatric Clinic, put it this way: *"What's done to children, they'll do to society."* What have you been contributing to society? What was done to you?

Appendix D is an example of normal parenting that—should have been done—to you.

WHICH GROUPS ARE YOU IN?

Some of you are teenagers discharged from foster care with little money, no income, poor education, no family or friends that can help you, and no marketable trade.

Some of you are in your fifties, sixties and seventies with little money, no income, poor education, no family or friends that can help you, and no marketable trade.

Some of you can only qualify to earn poverty wages.

Some of you are afraid to return to school.

Some of you define your life by who you hate.

Some of you are lazy.

Some of you are hard workers, but you do not have the training or skills to offer employers who want to pay you a living wage.

Some of you do not know what a living wage is.

Some of you do not read and write well.

Some of you believe employers owe you a job.

Some of you are ex-offenders reentering society.

Some of you are alcoholics.

Some of you are drug addicts.

Some of you are taking medications prescribed by a psychiatrist.

Some of you are veterans with an honorable discharge.

Some of you are veterans with less than an honorable discharge.

Some of you are single mothers.

Some of you are single fathers.

Some of you are families with children.

Some of you are married without children.

Some of you are victims of sexual abuse in your families.

Some of you are victims of physical and verbal abuse and neglect in your families.

Some of you have lived in poverty all of your lives.

Some of you receive government welfare payments.

Some of you call yourselves middle class because of pride, but you do not know what middle class is.

Some of you have never lived independent lives on your own.

Some of you have lived on your own income for less than five years out of your entire lives, but you talk about yourself as if you have always lived independently.

Some of you live in regret, shame and guilt.

Some of you live in anger and bitterness and are unforgiving.

Some of you need forgiveness.

Some of you fear success.

Some of you fear failure.

Some of you have been pretending so long you do not know what the facts are anymore.

Some of you are educated or trained and have worked successfully all of your lives—until now.

Some of you are HIV positive.

Some of you believe that all you need is a job and housing.

Some of you get jobs but cannot keep them.

Some of you are spoiled, and think people owe you a living.

Some of you believe the government, corporations and the economy are responsible for you being poor or homeless.

Some of you are waiting for the world to change so you can stop being poor or homeless.

Some of you are working as hard as you can to change your lives and succeed.

Some of you just do not care one way or the other.

Some of you think you already know all you need to know.

Some of you fear education.

Some of you are heterosexual, bisexual, homosexual, transgender, or other.

Some of you are African-Americans, Caucasians, Hispanics, Asians, Indians, Islanders, or other.

Some of you are Christians, Scientologists, Muslims, Jews, Buddhists, Atheist, or other.

Some of you begin your sentences with "My *only* problem is…"

Some of you are argumentative.

Some of you are passive and unmotivated.

Some of you are industrious, passionate and professional.

Some of you bite the hands that try to help you.

Some of you are kind, generous and loving.

Some of you are arrogant, selfish and mean.

Some of you are honest and trustworthy.

Some of you say one thing and do another.

Some of you are liars, thieves and manipulators.

Some of you are incapable of loving or being loved, with contempt for people in general and society as a whole.

Some of you believe you can do everything yourself and you do not need people.

Some of you refuse to learn, change, and grow.

Some of you want to learn, change, and grow, but you do not know how.

Some of you believe you have nothing to do with your own poverty or homelessness. It is just bad luck.

Overcome Being Poor or Homeless

Some of you think being poor in America is normal.

Some of you associate only with other poor people.

Some of you believe being beaten and humiliated as a child was normal.

Some of you are homeless.

All of you are poor.

THE NATURAL SUCCESS CYCLE OF LIFE

Change and growth immediately begin when a human sperm enters a human egg. If this automatic change and growth process stops, the embryo, or subsequent fetus, will die. The fastest growing part of the human body is the brain. Doctors tell us that the brain begins to learn in the womb. Therefore, they encourage parents to play music and talk to their child while it grows inside its mother. We do not teach babies to learn, change, and grow. It is natural for them to do so. **The natural success cycle of life for humans is to learn, change, and grow.**

If our natural success cycle of life stops after we are adults, then our bodies may live—but our dreams die.

If we are healthy, we continue to learn, change, and grow all of our life. For many of us this process is interrupted somewhere along the path of our life, neglected, or improperly nurtured and guided. The result is some kind of human dysfunction. If our physical learning, changing, and growing process is hampered, we will have a physical disability. Physical disabilities are usually visible and we know they exist. If our emotional learning, changing, and growing process is not good for us, then we will have character, attitude, and behavior dysfunctions in varying degrees of severity: from as mild as being inconsiderate of others to as severe as being a serial killer. Our character, attitude, and behavior dysfunctions are usually visible to other people—but not to us. We tend not to see our own blind spots unless we are searching for them, or another person, circumstance, or God, reveals them to us. These blind spots cause us to do things that are not in our own best interest.

Think back to the previous section entitled, "Which Groups Are You In?" Which groups did you identify with when you were reading it? For which ones did you say, "that's me" to yourself? Every group has blind spots. What are yours?

In 1865, Abraham Lincoln freed approximately 4 million African-American people from slavery in America. All of the people freed from those plantations were poor and homeless. It was illegal in America for hundreds of years to educate an enslaved person, so mass illiteracy prevailed. Those freed Black people not only were poor and homeless, they could not read and write. Because families were routinely sold and separated—with no letters from home—they left those plantations with nowhere to go. Not only that, there was no welfare, no food stamps, no downtown skid row missions, no health care, and no government mental health department transition team to ease their

Overcome Being Poor or Homeless

trauma of being dehumanized and brutalized for two hundred and forty-six years. They fought against hatred, robbery, rape, and random acts of murder, with almost no legal protections.

About seventy-five percent of them (3,000,000) chose to see an opportunity, got excited, got creative and discovered solutions. In spite of the horrible obstacles facing them, they became landowners, business owners, politicians, educators, tradesmen, scientist and professionals—and they even chose to change America. Within one hundred and forty-four years, less than two lifetimes, Barack Obama, an African-American, became President of the United States.

Look at what they accomplished, despite the evil they had to confront. Wow! How did they do it? They found something—inside themselves—that discovered solutions for them. They dared to learn, change, and grow, to overcome being poor and homeless.

The other twenty-five percent (1,000,000) felt threatened, or believed and acted like they were powerless. Even now, twenty-five percent remain poor and sometimes homeless.

Today, you do not have to suffer and contend, like those Africans in 1865 America, to succeed like them. On the contrary; the government, private foundations, corporations and individuals, are spending billions of dollars and employing millions of people—to protect your rights, give you legal aid, provide you medical and mental health care, feed you, clothe you, house you, give you spending money, help educate you and get you jobs and long term housing—so that you may have an opportunity to overcome being poor or homeless. Therefore, ask yourself this one question:

What do I need to learn, how do I need to change, and where do I need to grow, so I can overcome being poor or homeless?

Do not worry. The next sections will give you the ideas, tools, techniques and guidance you need to discover your answers. If you do not choose to pursue, persistently, your answers to these questions—then you are choosing to remain poor or homeless.

WHAT DO YOU NEED TO LEARN?

*"If there is no enemy within,
any enemy without can do us no harm"*
—African Proverb

First you must learn to examine yourself. To begin this process you have to practice thinking about what you are thinking. Two questions will help you:

1. What do I really want?
2. Is this in my best interest?

Notice that question one does not say, "What do I think I can get?" Nor does it ask, "What does my mother, father, friends, Roland Gilbert or any others, think I should want?" What do you really want? Your answer to this question is crucial to your success. In nearly every situation in your life, you need to take time to ask and answer it. Of course, if your life, or others, is in physical danger you may need to take immediate action. However, other than a life-threatening emergency, it is always wise to take time to ask and answer this question.

Immediately after you answer this question, ask yourself question two. Only you can determine what is in your best interest, because only you will pay the price, and receive the reward, for your choices. ***The truth is prices and rewards for our choices are inevitable.*** Everything we say, or fail to say, everything we do, or fail to do, and every thought we think, has prices and rewards. The ultimate question is always, "What prices am I willing to pay for the rewards I want?" African-Americans paid some serious prices—beatings, torture, murder—for the rewards they now enjoy. What about you? What prices are you willing to pay to get what you want?

Are you willing to pay the price of being kind to people who don't deserve it?

Are you willing to pay the price of being patient with yourself and patient with people who are impatient with you?

Are you willing to pay the price of giving respect to people in authority that you don't agree with?

Are you willing to pay the price of letting go of revenge and forgiving people who have hurt you?

Are you willing to pay the price of being dependable, responsible, and honest?

Are you willing to pay the price of keeping your word?

Are you willing to pay the price of asking people for help and good advice?

Are you willing to pay the price of receiving help and implementing good advice?

Are you willing to pay the price of being coachable?

Are you willing to pay the price of being friendly, sociable, and getting along with people?

Are you willing to pay the price of getting an education, so that you have a marketable trade to offer to employers in exchange for a living wage?

Are you willing to pay the price of hard work and persistence?

Are you willing to pay the price of helping others succeed and get what they want?

Are you willing to pay the price of looking for what you have to give others before you look for what they have to give you?

Are you willing to pay the price of doing whatever it takes, that is moral and legal, to get what you want?

Are you willing to pay the price to learn how to do what you have to do until you can do what you want to do?

Are you willing to pay the price to learn how to adapt, adjust, and move on?

Are you willing to pay the price to learn how?

Are you willing to pay the price to learn?

Are you willing to pay the price?

Are you willing to pay?

Are you willing?

Are you?

Practice makes improvement—that is the truth. There is no such thing as practice making perfect. I do not know who started that lie, but it simply is not true. Practice makes improvement—not perfect! We can always better our best. Every good professional knows this. That is why athletes, soldiers, entertainers, doctors, lawyers, teachers, mechanics, electricians and other high-quality professionals, continue to practice their trade—so they can get better at it. The Los Angeles Lakers know how to play basketball but they have a coach and are required to practice, consistently and habitually. United States Marines know how to fight, but they have commanders who make them practice, consistently and habitually.

Whenever people start to perform something they have not done before, a new task, they do it poorly. There are no exceptions to this rule. No matter how good you are, when you start something new, you will do it poorly compared to how well you will be doing it after years of practice. So please remember this truth: ***anything worth doing well is worth doing poorly***—until you get better at it.

You must be willing to pay the price of practicing, consistently and habitually, what you are learning. Daily practice of what you choose to learn is the only way you can change. Remember, there is no growth without change.

HOW DO YOU NEED TO CHANGE?

> *"I the LORD search the heart and examine the mind,*
> *to reward a man according to his conduct,*
> *according to what his deeds deserve."*
> Jeremiah 17:10
> The Holy Bible (NIV)

How do you talk to yourself and treat yourself? This is important because the truth is, **you cannot give what you do not have**. If your heart and mind do not value you, then your behavior will show it. Your behavior will show it towards yourself and others. Let us take a moment to look at your behavior towards your health, wealth, relationships, and self-expression.

Health

How you take care of your health affects your ability to succeed. The quality of your health affects your performance. If you smoke, eat unhealthy foods, and do not exercise, then you are choosing a low energy lifestyle which contributes to poor attendance, lack of focus and low motivation. Please take this seriously. Remember this truth: ***the most unselfish thing you can do is take care of yourself first, and then you will have more to give others.***

I recommend that you take off all your clothes and stand in front of a full-length mirror. Relax and let everything go. Now, look at yourself and ask yourself the two questions. Do you remember what they are? What do I really want? Is this in my best interest? Change often requires help. Please get the help you need to make the health changes you want.

Wealth

Wealth produces income. Wealth varies in amount and type. Welfare checks are a type of income that comes to you in small amounts. Jobs are a source of income in varying amounts. Stocks and bonds that pay dividends are another type of income that flows to you in various amounts. Gold is an asset, but it is not wealth because it does not produce income. You must sell the gold to get income. Once you sell it, then you no longer have it and it cannot produce anything for you anymore. The best type of wealth is income that flows to you independent of your daily direct efforts: like employee managed rental property, certain types of business investments, patents, copyrights, royalties, and any other thing that produces an income for you.

The amount of income you receive is crucial. It determines if you are poor or not. If you want to overcome being poor, you must know what the correct amount of income is for you. This amount will vary, depending on your individual circumstances and requirements: the housing cost in your area, the number of children living with you, the expenses required for your lifestyle, etc. You must know the minimum amount of income required for you to avoid poverty. If you do not know this number, then you run the risk of working your way into poverty. You can get help to calculate this number. There are many public social service agencies, community programs, churches, and volunteer services at your local library that can help you. Once you have this number you will know your individual living wage.

Your living wage is the minimum amount of income—you must have—so you can live independent of public charity.

It is OK to take a job that pays you less than your living wage if you are receiving some public support, like Section 8 Housing Vouchers or Food Stamps. Do what you have to do until you can do what you want to do. However, please know that you will remain poor until you earn your living wage or more. Therefore, your goal should always be to answer this question: ***What do I need to learn, how do I need to change, and what do I need to do to prepare myself to earn my living wage?***

Ask yourself this question daily, regardless of any job you have, as long as you are poor. Daily, talk to people who can help you answer this question. In addition to any other people you choose, I recommend that you also talk to counselors at your local community colleges. It does not matter that you did poorly in school, or did not graduate high school. It also does not matter how old you are. You can be another two years older—*without* a marketable trade—or you can be two years older—*with* a marketable trade. You will still be two years older, either way—right? So talk to some college counselors anyway. They can help you.

I also recommend you read the book, "Think & Grow Rich: The Landmark Bestseller—Now Revised and Updated for The 21st Century," by Napoleon Hill and Arthur Pell, ISBN-13: 978-1585424337.

Your living wage job may not be your career. You need to have a trade or skill you can always rely on to keep you independent and off public charity. Take the time to learn a marketable trade—first. Then pursue your career, your dreams and your greatness. This is another truth to remember: ***a job is a temporary inconvenience on the way to your greatness.***

There are different ways to discover your greatness. As part of my mission, I teach people how to build their own Integrity Structure. Your Integrity Structure is the foundation and framework of your greatness. It answers five questions: Who am I? What do I really want that death cannot destroy? What does my life promise to leave behind after I die? What is my purpose in life? What is my mission in life? In my book, "Power Parenting for Poor People," I show you, step by step, how to build your Integrity Structure for your greatness, and also teach you how to do it for your children's greatness.

Everyone has some gift to give to society. The gift you have to give people will always provide you a living wage, or more. Find it and give it, because the true secret of success is to help other people get what they want. Help people get what they want, and someone will pay you for it. How can you help people? Until you find your gift, your greatness, remember that a living wage job can be a temporary inconvenience on the way to your greatness. Because people are the key to your success, the quality of your relationships is vital.

Relationships

We come into this world naked and without material goods. Everything we get must come from other people. If not, we die. As we grow, we continue to get what we need from other people. As this process continues throughout our life, we take our turn and become sources for other people. The normal human life cycle is, first, we receive what we need from people, and then we give people what they need. There is no such thing as, "pulling yourself up by your own boot straps." Everybody gets help. We all need each other.

We have three main categories of relationships. We have a relationship with our self, with our God, and with our environment. Other people, of course, are part of our environment.

How we talk to ourselves determines the quality of our relationships. How do you talk to yourself? Do you call yourself ugly, slow, dumb, loser, stupid, and no good? Do you use profane words to describe yourself? Do you call yourself by degrading animal names, like cow, heifer, snake, and dog? You must say things to yourself and about yourself that are positive and encouraging.

What is your internal conversation with your higher power? Are you in conflict, confusion, or strife with God? If you do not have peace with your higher power, then deal with it immediately. There is plenty of help all around you. Settle this matter now—do not put this off—because your life depends on it. You must be at peace with God in order to prosper in all areas of your life.

How do you talk to yourself about other people? What words do you use to describe them? Do you use words that say other people are more valuable, or less valuable, than you are? Do your words about other people show fear, envy, selfishness, bitterness or resentment? People sense how you feel about them, regardless of how you might pretend. Talk to yourself about other people with words that reflect kindness, compassion, mercy, forgiveness and love.

Choose your friends wisely. ***Either our relationships support our success or they support our failure. Do the people you choose to have close to you contribute to your success or to your failure?***

Stop expressing yourself with profanity.

Self-expression

What do you love to do that expresses you? What is your thing? For me, it is teaching my workshops to help people heal the pain of their past, see their blind spots, discover and cultivate their greatness. You can sense when a person is doing the thing that expresses them. When you watch an athlete, politician, police officer, bus driver, receptionist, teacher, preacher, postal worker, server, cook, mother, soldier, bricklayer, or anyone doing a job—you can tell the difference between those who love it and those who are just doing it—can't you?

Here are four criteria to help you find the thing you do that expresses you:

1. Your must love to do it.
2. It must help other people in some way.
3. You would do it for no money (Even though you might make lots of money doing it.)
4. You tend to lose track of time when you do it.

Your true self-expression will meet all four requirements at once. Some people find their thing in music, art, fixing mechanical things, homemaking, counseling, coaching or in many other types of endeavors.

Balance is a key! Change without balance is a tragedy waiting to happen. I am sure you are already familiar with numerous celebrity stories of self-destruction, from Elvis Presley or Michael Jackson, to politicians and corporate CEO's. Many celebrities have fulfilled their self-expression and wealth. Their relationships and their health, however, suffer from neglect and addictions, which lead to broken families, prison, sickness and death. Their lives are out of balance.

We have two currencies to spend in life, one is time and the other is money. Money you can spend, or lose, and get more of it. Time, however, you cannot. Every hour you spend is gone forever. There is no such thing as making up time. You are always using new time because you only have so much time allotted for your life. You will die. Therefore, the most important currency you have to spend is time. Spend your time and money in balance on your health, wealth, relationships, and self-expression. You will be glad you did.

Know this truth: ***balance in all things is a key to peace and happiness.*** As you learn and change, balance is a key to your healthy growth. Stay in balance as you learn, change, and grow.

WHERE DO YOU NEED TO GROW?

> *"No problem can be solved from the same level of consciousness that created it."*
> ——Albert Einstein

Human growth means to get better at living life. Growth is a process of expansion—expanding our experiences, knowledge, understanding and wisdom. Growth is seeing yourself and the world around you in new and better ways. Growth is seeing yourself and your circumstances with the hope of what can be, rather than focusing on the limits of your condition. When you choose to do this, then you are raising your consciousness. When you raise your consciousness, then you discover new solutions. Answers come to you beyond what you already know. Isn't this what those African-Americans who left those plantations—illiterate, poor, and homeless—did to succeed in hostile circumstances?

Only the truth will set you free. The following life truths will contribute to your continuing growth.

The fruit comes from the root. Your adult behaviors reflect what happened to you while you were growing up. What happened to you was not your fault. However, it is now your responsibility to do something about it. Please get the help you need to overcome your dysfunctional behaviors. You probably already know what some of them are; now is the time to deal with them. Reread the previous section entitled, "Which Groups Are You In?" This section will help you identify some dysfunctional behaviors that might be blind spots for you. **What you don't know can hurt you.** Please ask people you respect to go over the list with you, to help you discover what you might be missing about yourself. I am sure you will find people who will tell you the truth.

Hurt people, hurt people. People, who are hurt, hurt other people. The people who hurt you in your life were not full of love, peace, joy, patience, kindness, goodness, faithfulness, gentleness, and self-control. They were hurt themselves in some way. If you knew the truth of their childhood, then you would probably understand them better. We are all hurt in some way, and we all pass our hurt on to others in some way. Please remember: *you cannot give what you do not have.* They gave you what they had to give. Apply this life truth to yourself as well—because, I am sure, you have also hurt some people along the way.

Forgiveness is for giving. Forgiveness is forgiving; and forgiveness is for giving. The purpose of forgiveness is to give it away. If people have to earn our forgiveness then we are not forgiving them, because they would have earned it. If a person earns something then we owe it to them.

Forgiveness comes from our hearts and is a gift we give to others. Forgiveness does not mean you have to be around the person you forgive—please take care of yourself. Make the choice to do what is best for others and for you. Forgive, so that you can also be forgiven (Matthew 6:14-15).

True love is choosing to give people what is best for them. Please notice that true love is not about what you need, want, or can get. True love is not about you. It is all about others. Appendix D is an example of true love. Wouldn't you love to have someone love you this way? Try giving true love to others first, and then wait and see what comes back to you. I am sure you will be pleasantly surprised. Sometimes what is best for people is for you to let them go and not be around them. Bishop T. D. Jakes speaks on, "Let It Go," in Appendix C. Remember, however, that balance is always a key to everything we do.

Life is not fair—get over it—stay focused on what you want. Hurricanes, tornadoes, earthquakes, tsunamis, diseases, accidents, wars, famines and bad decisions happen. There are people who will not like you and will treat you unfairly. There are people who will like you but will treat you unfairly. There are people who will not care about you one way or another, and will treat you unfairly. Yes, there is evil in the world. Get over it. These things happen. Do not talk to people about what they did not do for you. Talk to people about what they can do, **_now_**, to help you get more of what you want. Do not sacrifice getting results for being right about how wrong someone is. Learn to adapt, adjust, and move on.

Power is taking 100% responsibility for how you think, feel, and act. Responsibility means the ability to respond. It does not mean whose is at fault or who is to blame. When you take responsibility, you are not admitting guilt—you are responding to what has happened. Life is happening all the time. You cannot stop life. You cannot control life. Every morning when you open your eyes you step into life. Life is whatever it is for you at that moment. You have a choice. You can choose to let your circumstance dictate how you think, feel, and act about what you are facing, or you can choose how you want to respond. Do you want to respond to life in a way that gets you more of what you want? You can, because it is your choice.

If you woke up on freedom day in 1865 on that plantation, how would you choose to think, feel, and act about it? Would you choose to see how unfair it all is, your lack of preparation, education, money, protection, and all the dangers you must contend with that make your situation hopeless? Or would you choose to see an opportunity and get excited about your potential and what is possible for you? The choice is always yours.

Use your power to see an opportunity, get excited, get creative and discover solutions in every situation in your life.

You do not believe what you see, you see what you believe. Our eyes are lenses that capture light and images and project them onto our brain. Our eyes do not see, our brain sees. Is a glass of water half-full or half empty? What you see depends on what you believe. Can a man be dependable, trustworthy, a leader, a protector, one who keeps you safe? What you see depends on what you believe. Can a woman be trustworthy, honest, respectful, a nurturer, one to whom you can safely express your real thoughts and feelings? What you see depends on what you believe. Will a police officer, politician, your caseworker, your boss, do the right thing? What you see depends on what you believe. Are your current circumstances hopeless or full of potential and possibilities?

Givers gain. Imagine going to the mountains in the winter to enjoy the snow. You walk into your cabin, go over to the fireplace and then say, "OK, I'm cold, give me some heat, and then I will go outside and chop you some wood!" Of course, it does not work that way. Life does not work that way either. You must give first. Therefore, at your school, job, business, in your family, or wherever you work with people, always look for what you can give first. Your returns will be greater than what you gave. Do not be surprised if your blessing comes back to you from a different person, or source, than you originally gave to.

Self-respect does not come from other people. If you know who you really are then you do not have to prove it to others. When no one else is around you, you are never lonely—if you like the person you are alone with. No one has the power to disrespect you unless you give it to him or her. How do you give it to them? You give other people the power to disrespect you when you choose to believe that what they say about you is more important than what you say about yourself. Please tell yourself the following two statements as needed: *Just because you say it, does not make it true. What you think about me is not more important than what I think about myself.*

Persistence means you never stop until you win. To overcome being poor, you must choose every day to persist. I cannot say this any better than others have already said it.

"Nothing in the world can take the place of persistence. Talent will not; nothing is more common than unsuccessful men with talent. Genius will not; unrewarded genius is almost a proverb. Education will not; the world is full of educated derelicts. Persistence and determination are omnipotent. The slogan 'press on' has solved and always will solve the problems of the human race. No person was ever honored for what he received. Honor has been the reward for what he gave."
——(John) Calvin Coolidge

Overcome Being Poor or Homeless

"If I had to select one quality, one personal characteristic that I regard as being most highly correlated with success, whatever the field, I would pick the trait of persistence. Determination. The will to endure to the end, to get knocked down seventy times and get up off the floor saying, 'Here comes number seventy-one!'"

———Richard M. Devos

"Failure is only postponed success as long as courage coaches ambition. The habit of persistence is the habit of victory."

———Herbert Kaufman

"I am personally convinced that one person can be a change catalyst, a 'transformer' in any situation, any organization. Such an individual is yeast that can leaven an entire loaf. It requires vision, initiative, patience, respect, persistence, courage, and faith to be a transforming leader."

———Stephen R. Covey

"Energy and persistence conquer all things."

———Benjamin Franklin

"Studies indicate that the one quality all successful people have is persistence. They're willing to spend more time accomplishing a task and to persevere in the face of many difficult odds. There's a very positive relationship between people's ability to accomplish any task and the time they're willing to spend on it."

———Dr. Joyce Brothers

"Persistence is the twin sister of excellence. One is a matter of quality; the other, a matter of time."

———Marabel Morgan

"Never let your persistence and passion turn into stubbornness and ignorance."

———Anthony J. D'Angelo

"Patience, persistence and perspiration make an unbeatable combination for success."

———Napoleon Hill

"Keep on asking, and you will be given what you ask for. Keep on looking, and you will find. Keep on knocking, and the door will be opened. For everyone who asks, receives. Everyone who seeks, finds. And the door is opened to everyone who knocks."

———Jesus Christ
Matthew 7:7–8
The Holy Bible (NLT)

HOW TO GET BETTER RESULTS FROM SOCIAL SERVICE AGENCIES

Our federal government grants money to states, county and city governments, and agencies, to help poor and homeless people. Many different federal government departments make these grants. For example, the Department of Health and Human Services, Department of Housing and Urban Development, Department of Veterans Affairs, and others. Some of these government departments also make competitive awards directly to nonprofit organizations to help the poor and the homeless. Private foundations also give money to help the poor and the homeless. Every year, the government, foundations and individual donors, spend billions of dollars to help the poor and the homeless in America.

The Los Angeles Department of Public Social Services annual budget is over $3 billion dollars and they have more than 13,000 employees. The Los Angeles Homeless Services Authority, in fiscal year 2011, spent over $118 million funding more than 380 different community programs.

The agencies you go to for help are huge, complex bureaucracies. The smaller community agencies that service you, including skid row missions, get their money from these larger government bureaucracies, foundations, and public and private donors. The money usually comes with performance requirements. If they want to keep their jobs, they must accomplish the performance requirements demanded by the funders. This is where a major problem occurs—for you.

The United States Department of Health and Human Services, in fiscal year 2011, was a $1.3 trillion agency with over 65,000 employees. *"Our mission is to enhance the health and well-being of Americans by providing for effective health and human services and by fostering sound, sustained advances in the sciences, underlying medicine, public health, and social services."*

Please notice that their job is to provide you social services. It is not their job to eliminate your poverty.

The United States Department of Housing and Urban Development, in fiscal year 2011, was a $45 billion agency with about 10,000 employees. *"HUD's mission is to create strong, sustainable, inclusive communities and quality affordable homes for all. HUD is working to strengthen the housing market to bolster the economy and protect consumers; meet the need for quality affordable rental homes: utilize housing as a platform for improving quality of life; build inclusive and sustainable communities free from discrimination; and transform the way HUD does business."*

Please notice that their job is to provide you housing services. It is not their job to eliminate your poverty.

Overcome Being Poor or Homeless

The United States Department of Veterans Affairs spent more than $118 billion, in fiscal year 2011, and had approximately 280,000 full-time equivalent employees. *"The mission of VA is to fulfill President Lincoln's promise – 'To care for him who shall have borne the battle, and for his widow, and his orphan'– by serving and honoring the men and women who are America's Veterans."*

Please notice that their job is to provide you services. It is not their job to eliminate your poverty.

The Los Angeles Homeless Services Authority's mission is, *"To support, create and sustain solutions to homelessness in Los Angeles County by providing leadership, advocacy, planning, and management of program funding."*

Please notice that their job is to provide you employment and housing services. If you get any type of housing, any type of employment, and are still poor, and receiving food stamps, housing subsidies, and other forms of public charity—then they have completed their mission. It is not their job to eliminate your poverty.

The Los Angeles Department of Public Social Services' mission is, *"To enrich lives through effective and caring service."*

Please notice that their job is to provide you services. It is not their job to eliminate your poverty.

All of the billions of dollars and thousands of employees are working to provide you a safety net of services for the trapeze act of life. They are not working, however, to put you back on the trapeze. Therefore, *if you are not working to overcome being poor—then no one is working for you to overcome being poor.*

Remember, to overcome being poor you must have, at least, a living wage income that keeps you off public welfare. I do not know of any government money, foundation money, community organization money, or donor money, whose performance requirement is—*the number of people who earn a living wage and no longer receive public charity.*

(Social Security is not public charity. Social Security is money taken from our paychecks plus a matching amount taken from our employers. Social Security is an interest free loan we are forced to give to the federal government—and hope we get some of it back before we die.)

The performance requirements demanded by the funders are where a major problem occurs—for you. The organizations helping you are doing what they are funded to do. The funders want to help you—they do not want to do it for you. You need their help. You, however, are one hundred percent responsible for using all the resources available to you so—*you* can overcome being poor.

Every time you talk with that social service person at the counter, behind the window, at their desk, at your door, or on the phone, please remember something. They want to help you. However, they did not write the policies and rules they must follow. These things come down through the organization to them. Sometimes the employee you are speaking with does not fully agree with what they are saying to you—but they are part of the team and must comply. Sometimes the employee lacks complete and accurate information about their own organization, as well as how other organizations can help you. Sometimes, these conditions get the best of the employee and they become frustrated, feel powerless, and direct it at you. Please forgive them and be patient. Please be kind to them. Kindness is choosing to be courteous to people who, you think, may not deserve it. Please stay focused on the two questions—getting more of what you want, and doing what is in your own best interest.

In order to access the hundreds of programs and billions of dollars available to help you, you must talk to people. After that, you must talk to more people. No one knows all the programs available to help poor and homeless people in America. It sounds amazing, but it is true. A good place to start your search is your local public library. Go to the reference librarian and tell them what you want. You want the names, addresses and phone numbers of all the programs in your city that help poor people. After you find out what a particular organization can, or cannot, do to help you, always ask that person to give you the names of any other programs they know. Talk to people and then, talk to more people. Please remember, persistence always succeeds. So keep on asking, seeking, and knocking.

7 DAILY HABITS TO OVERCOME BEING POOR

1. Listen to your thoughts.

2. Ask yourself, "Will my current thoughts get me more of what I want?"

3. Choose to think thoughts that get you more of what you want.

4. Listen to what you say.

5. Choose to say words that get you more of what you want.

6. To think is to create: What you *believe* and *speak* becomes true for you. You do not believe what you see—you see what you believe! What have I *believed* and *said* in the past to create my current reality? What do I need to *believe* and *say* now—to create the future I want?

7. Choose to DIE. **Desire** means to crave something. Hold your breath for as long as you can. That first breath is not optional. You crave it. You desire it. Daily you must desire to overcome being poor. **Imagination** means to form mental images or pictures of what is not actually present—yet. You do this all the time: with things, food you want to eat, places you want to go, and people you want to be with. Now do it daily for the life you want to live without being poor. **Expectation** means to know something is going to

happen. Every time you sit in a chair, you do not question if that chair will hold you. You do not take time to inspect the chair. You just sit down. Likewise, know you will overcome being poor. Just do it daily.

You have much more to work with than those Africans who left those plantations in 1865 and fought to become Americans. Nevertheless, today, you can still use what they used to overcome being poor and homeless. They told themselves—words. The words they chose created overcoming—thoughts. Their thoughts created courageous—feelings. Their feelings created confident—decisions. Their decisions created bold—actions. Their actions created successful—habits. Their habits created a persistent—character. Their character created a victorious—destiny.

Yes, you can—overcome being poor—if you choose to.
I love you.

RECOMMENDED RESOURCES

Power Parenting for Poor People, by Roland J. Gilbert, ISBN-13: 978-1491261248.

The Drama of the Gifted Child, The Search for the True Self, by Alice Miller, ISBN-13: 978-0465016907.

www.biblestudytools.com

Raising Black Children: Two Leading Psychiatrists Confront the Educational, Social and Emotional Problems Facing Black Children, by James P. Comer, MD and Alvin F. Poussaint, MD. ISBN-13: 978-0452268395.

Believer's Voice of Victory Magazine, for free subscription write to Kenneth Copeland Ministries, Fort Worth, Texas 76192-0001, or sign up online at www.kcm.org, or call 800-575-4455.

The Citizens Commission on Human Rights, www.cchr.org. 1-800-869-2247.

Think & Grow Rich: The Landmark Bestseller—Now Revised and Updated for The 21st Century, by Napoleon Hill and Arthur Pell, ISBN-13: 978-1585424337.

Life Without Limbs: The Nick Vujicic Story. www.lifewithoutlimbs.org

APPENDIX A
SOME TRUTHS IN THIS BOOK

- The natural success cycle of life for humans is to learn, change, and grow.
- Prices and rewards for our choices are inevitable.
- Practice makes improvement.
- Anything worth doing well is worth doing poorly.
- You cannot give what you do not have.
- The most unselfish thing you can do is take care of yourself first, and then you will have more to give others.
- What do I need to learn, how do I need to change, and what do I need to do to prepare myself to earn my living wage?
- A job is a temporary inconvenience on the way to your greatness.
- Either our relationships support our success or they support our failure. Do the people you choose to have close to you contribute to your success or to your failure?
- The true secret of success is to help other people get what they want.
- Balance in all things is a key to peace and happiness.

- The fruit comes from the root.
- What you don't know can hurt you.
- Hurt people, hurt people.
- Forgiveness is for giving.
- True love is choosing to give people what is best for them.
- Life is not fair—get over it—stay focused on what you want.
- Power is taking 100% responsibility for how you think, feel, and act.
- You do not believe what you see, you see what you believe.
- Givers gain.
- Self-respect does not come from other people.
- Persistence means you never stop until you win.
- If you are not working to overcome being poor—then no one is working for you to overcome being poor.

APPENDIX B
SOME PEOPLE WHO OVERCAME BEING POOR AND HOMELESS

Halle Berry . . . **Oscar-winning** and **Emmy Award-winning** actress (shelter in New York City) (sources: *Reader's Digest*, April 2007, cover story: "Halle Berry: From homeless shelter to Hollywood fame." Page: 89: RD: "Is it true that when you moved to New York to begin your acting career, you lived in a shelter?" Berry: "Very briefly. ...I wasn't working for a while. RD: "How old were you then?" Berry: "I probably was about 21. But a girl had to do what a girl had to do. You can do that when you're 21 and ambitious, and your eyes are this big and you don't want to go home." / *US* magazine, April 22, 2007: "Halle Berry was homeless. Berry slept at a shelter in NYC after her mom refused to send her money.").

Daniel Craig . . . actor; James Bond in the 007 movies (park bench in London while a struggling actor). (source: *Daily Mail* newspaper, October 14, 2005).

David Letterman . . . **Emmy Award-winning** television writer-comedian; talk-show host; American author (host of the television talk-show *Late Show with David Letterman*) (red 1973 Chevy pickup truck).

Phil McGraw / "Dr. Phil" . . . TV talk show host; **best-selling American author**; former psychologist (age 12, Kansas City, Kansas USA, after he and his father moved there while the elder McGraw interned as a psychologist) (source: *Globe* tabloid newspaper, June 22, 2009, pg 42, "Dirt Poor Dr. Phil Lived in a Car!": "TV shrink Dr. Phil McGraw is a multimillionaire now, but as a youth, he was so poor, he was homeless and living in a car. ... 'I was homeless living in a car with my dad. We eventually got a room at the downtown YMCA for five bucks a week...").

John Paul DeJoria . . . **Billionaire** American businessman; co-founder and spokesperson of the hair-care company "John Paul Mitchell Systems" (homeless twice in his early 20s as a single father in Los Angeles).

Jim Carrey . . . actor-writer-producer-comedian (yellow VW van in various Canadian locations with older brother **John Carrey**, older sister **Rita Carrey**, and parents **Percy Carrey** and **Kathleen Carrey**/outdoor camping in a tent with his family in the backyard of the home of his older married sister, Patricia Carrey).

Sylvester Stallone . . . **Oscar-winning** actor and screenwriter; film director-producer (Port Authority bus station in New York City) (source: *Total Film* magazine, August 2010, page 111: "I was broke and basically sleeping in the Port Authority bus station for three weeks straight. I read in a trade paper about this film [*The Party at Kitty and Studs"*, 1970] that was paying $100 a day—for a $100 a day I would wreak havoc. Instead of doing something desperate, I worked for two days for $200 and got myself out of the bus station.").

Tyler Perry . . . actor-director-writer-producer; playwright (car: Geo Metro convertible in the mid 1990s in Atlanta, Georgia USA) (source: *Best Life* magazine, April 2008, cover story: "A Longer, Richer Life: How Tyler Perry Went From Living in His Car to Commanding a $500 Million Enterprise.

Tupac Shakur . . . actor; rap music star (homeless shelters).

Overcome Being Poor or Homeless

"Colonel" Harland Sanders . . . businessman; entrepreneur; founder-spokesperson of the "Kentucky Fried Chicken" fast-food restaurant chain (homeless at age 10 when his mother remarried and he left home due to altercations with his stepfather/car as an adult; slept in the backseat nightly because he could not afford lodging as he traveled around the United States and Canada, sometimes with his wife Claudia, trying to sign up restaurants to use his special fried chicken recipe for a franchise licensing fee).

Chris Gardner . . . Multimillionaire stockbroker; American author; the 2006 movie *the Pursuit of Happyness* starring Wil Smith was based on his life (subway stations, trains, bathrooms, church-run shelter with his son in California).

William Shatner . . . **Emmy Award-winning** actor-director; **best-selling Canadian-born American author** (pick-up truck with a walk-in camper on the back for a time after his divorce due to financial difficulties after the cancellation of the television series *Star Trek*, in which he starred. Included in that time was traveling the east coast of the U.S. appearing in a play on the summer theater circuit and sleeping in the camper with his dog, a Doberman pinscher. Shatner: "I now had three children and an ex-wife to support and I was just about broke. I even lived out of a pick-up truck for a while." Source: DailyMail.co.uk, May 11, 2008 / Shatner: "I lived out of the back of my truck, under a hard shell. It had a little stove, a toilet, and I'd drive from theater to theater. The only comfort came from my dog, who sat in the passenger seat and gave me perspective on everything." Source: *Details* magazine, January 2008. / Shatner: "I'd been a working actor for decades, I'd starred in three failed TV series [*Star Trek* the most recent] , and I was a divorced father of three children living in the back of a truck." Source: book: *Up Until Now: The Autobiography*, by William Shatner with David Fisher, 2008, page 159. / Also, earlier in his life, he hitchhiked across the U.S. with a male friend during a summer break after their freshman year in college. Source: from the same above autobiography, page 32: "We had no money, so we made signs reading 'Two mcGill Freshman Seeing the U.S.' and hit the road. We spent three months living in cars and sleeping on the grass and on the beach.")

Jean-Claude Van Damme . . . actor (Los Angeles streets) (source: *The Sun*, UK newspaper, Feb 6, 2009, interview, Van Damme: "My eldest son doesn't know how to deal with society because I over-protect him because of my last life of being on the street and sleeping on the street and starving in L.A. I didn't want him to have that.").

Hilary Swank . . . **Oscar-winning** actress (car, an Oldsmobile/one of two air mattresses on the floor of a friend's vacant house at age 15-16 with her mother after the two moved to Los Angeles from Washington state by car). (source, among others: *Reader's Digest*, January 2007, cover story: "Hilary Swank: How Her Risky Choice Paid Off" Page 102: "In 1989, when she was 15, Swank and her mom packed up their Oldsmobile Delta 88 and, with just $75, headed to Los Angeles. They lived in the car until a friend gave them a place to stay. Swank's mom used a pay phone to book her daughter for auditions.")

Joan Rivers . . . **Emmy Award-winning** television talk-show host; TV-radio show host; **best-selling American author**; comedienne (car).

Kelly Clarkson . . . **Grammy Award-winning** singer; *American Idol* television talent show 1st-season winner 2002 (car/shelter, with her female roommate after a major structural fire forced them out of a 71-unit apartment building in West Hollywood, California in March 2002) (source: *Inside Edition* television newsmagazine, September 5,

2002; story/interview with her roommate-fellow Texan, actress-singer-dancer Janet Harvick. Janet: "It was really, really rough because we had just moved here, and we had just moved in the day of the fire. We knew nobody here—I mean nobody, so the night of the fire, the next day, and night, we stayed in our car." / *US Weekly* magazine, September 23, 2002; print story: "'My apartment [building] burned down; my car got towed twice,' recalls Clarkson, who, with nowhere to go, lived in a homeless shelter for several days.").

Kelsey Grammer . . . Emmy Award-winning actor (star of the television series *Frasier*) (outdoor camping in back of a theater behind his motorcycle) (source: *Entertainment Tonight*, December 12, 2001, celebrity "Rags to Riches" story segment, snippet from a 1994 *ET* sit-down interview).

Shania Twain . . . Grammy Award-winning singer (homeless shelter in Toronto, Canada in 1979 at age 14 with her mother and siblings; then alone for a time at age 16 in 1981, squatting in a vacant house and sleeping on a bus, also in Toronto) (sources: autobiography *From This Moment On* by Shania Twain, 2011, page 14, 16: "Ten hours later, we reached Toronto. Mom got out of the car to use a pay phone while we sat and waited in the car, returning a few minutes later with a piece of paper on which she'd scribbled the address of a homeless shelter. That night, the five of us slept in a crowded, sweltering place on cot-like beds . . ." / biography: *Shania Twain: The Biography* by Robin Eggar, 2005; Shania: "We drove to Toronto and went to a shelter. We finally got fed every day.").

Sally Jessy Raphael . . . Emmy Award-winning television talk-show host; American author (car).

Martin Sheen . . . **Emmy Award-winning** actor-director-producer (New York City subway while a young struggling actor).

Drew Carey . . . **Emmy Award-nominated** actor-writer-producer-comedian; television game show host; **best-selling American author** (car) (source: *Entertainment Tonight*, May 23, 2002; birthdays segment, co-host Mary Hart: "Which star of *The Drew Carey Show* once lived out of his car? That's Drew Carey himself, who turns 44 today.")

Kurt Cobain . . . **Grammy Award-winning** singer-songwriter-musician; rock star; lead vocalist of the band "Nirvana" (outdoor camping under a bridge in Aberdeen, Washington USA/cardboard box on the porch of a drummer friend/hallway floor of an apartment building/hospital waiting room/old couch in a garage). (source: book, *Heavier Than Heaven: A Biography of kurt Cobain*, by Charles R. Cross, 2001).

Lil' Kim . . . **Grammy Award-winning** rap singer; actress (car, for a time during her youth with her mother).

Jim Morrison . . . singer-songwriter; poet; lead singer and lyricist for the 1960s rock band "The Doors"; Rock and Roll Hall of Fame inductee (with The Doors) (rooftops/cars/under the pier at Venice Beach, California/friends' couches).

Frenchie Davis . . . singer; *American Idol* television talent show 2nd-season semifinalist contestant; *Entertainment Tonight* special correspondent (homeless for three months; stayed with friends) (sources: *Entertainment Tonight*, February 12, 2003; *Us Weekly* magazine, March 3-10, 2003).

Jacqueline Danforth . . . daughter of television journalist Barbara Walters and theatrical producer Lee

Guber; founder-executive director of Daughters, Inc. / New Horizons Wilderness Program for young women (ran away from home in 1984 at age 15 and hitchhiked approximately 800 miles across the southwest United States for a month) (source: *Dateline NBC* TV newsmagazine, October 18, 2002, Jackie Danforth and Barbara Walters oncamera interview conducted by host Jane Pauley. Jackie: "I ended up hitchhiking with some guy that I, you know, met on the street. And he [eventually] went through my wallet and found a phone number." Barbara: "And he called me. And then I knew where she was, thank God.").

Jewel . . . **Grammy Award-nominated** singer-songwriter (1979 VW van; joined eventually by her mother/manager Lenedra Carroll, who lived out of her own VW van. Jewel: "I was homeless when I was 18." (quote source: *TV Guide* magazine, March 16-22, 2009, pg 9).

Suze Orman . . . **best-selling American author**; fiancial advisor (van) (source: *Current Biography Yearbook 2003*, page 395: "She ended her travels in Berkeley, California, working there as a tree cutter and living in a Ford van).

Benjamin Franklin . . . one of the Founding Fathers of the United States; one of the authors of the Declaration of Independence; **best-selling American author**, statesman, printer, scientist, inventor, philosopher (ran away from home in Boston at age 17 via a ship journey to New York City, then made his way to Philadelphia on foot and by boat) (source, his autobiography: *Memoires De La Vie Privee*, published in 1791, a year after his death: "So I sold some of my books to raise a little money, was taken on board privately, and as we had a fair wind, in three days I found myself in New York, near three hundred miles from home, a boy of but seventeen, without the least recommendation to or knowledge of any person in the place, and with very little money in my pocket.").

Nathaniel Ayers . . . classical street musician; musical prodigy; subject of the book and 2009 film *The Soloist* starring Robert Downey Jr. and Jamie Foxx as Ayers. ("Skid Row" in Los Angeles; developed schizophrenia during his second year of training at Juilliard School).

John Drew Barrymore . . . actor; father of actress Drew Barrymore (streets/shelters).

Matthew Ansara . . . actor; son of actress Barbara Eden and actor Michael Ansara (car in the Los Angeles area at age 19 after his parents found out he had not been attending or even registered at college as he had claimed) (sources: Barbara Eden autobiography *Jeannie Out of the Bottle*, 2011, by Barbara Eden with Wendy Leigh, page 250, Eden: "Eventually we were able to discover that Matthew had been living partly on the streets and partly with a friend who'd taken him in out of pity." / *20/20 Downtown*, ABC-TV newsmagazine, January 30, 2002, Barbara Eden oncamera sit-down interview conducted by Connie Chung. / *People* magazine, March 11, 2002, Barbara Eden print interview.).

Danny Bonaduce . . . actor; radio-show host; American author (car, just before beginning his radio career).

Heather Mills . . . British model-television presenter; author; humanitarian; divorced wife of singer-songwriter Paul McCartney (outdoor camping at London's Waterloo train station at age 14).

Charlie Chaplin . . . **Oscar-winning** actor-writer-director-producer; British-born author; **knighted** (streets of London during his childhood after his father died and his mother suffered a mental breakdown).

D-Vine . . . rap music star (homeless shelter after his mother died).

Troy Donahue . . . actor (temporary shelters/outdoor camping in Central Park in New York City).

George Eads . . . actor (one of the stars of the television series *CSI: Crime Scene Investigation*) (car, in Los Angeles while a struggling actor).

John Green Brady (John G. Brady) . . . governor of Alaska 1897-1906 (streets of New York City during his childhood; sent west on one of many "orphan trains," accompanied on this particular trip by future North Dakota governor Andrew Burke).

Andrew Burke . . . governor of North Dakota 1870-1873 (streets of New York City during his childhood; sent west on one of many "orphan trains," accompanied on this particular trip by future Alaska governor John Green Brady).

Carmen Electra . . . actress; model; American author (early 20s, Los Angeles area after her boyfriend stole her savings) (source: *Las Vegas Review-Journal*, "Homeless days helped shape Carmen Electra," by Doug Elfman, July 6, 2009; Electra: "'You know, I had a couple of years of being homeless in Hollywood,' Electra tells me. 'A lot of people don't even know this.' She was in her early 20s back then. ... 'I remember sitting on a park bench in the valley,' she says. 'I was crying because I was stranded. It was over 100 degrees outside.'").

Ella Fitzgerald . . . **Grammy Award-winning** singer; **U.S. Presidential Medal of Freedom** recipient (streets of Harlem in New York City for a year while a teenager just before she won an amateur singing talent contest at the Apollo Theater).

Richard Fagan . . . American songwriter; has written six number-one hit songs and albums featuring his songs have sold over 25 million copies (homeless twice in the 1970s after being discharged from military service in the Vietnam War).

John Garfield . . . **Oscar-nominated** actor (outdoor camping/freight trains).

Harry Houdini . . . magician; escape artist; paranormal investigator; Hungarian-born American author (streets/outdoor camping/temporary shelters; left home at age 12 in search of work and traveled for two years on his own, making his way from Wisconsin to Missouri and settling finally in New York City).

Lionel Aldridge . . . American football player; television sportscaster-analyst; played in two winning Super Bowl games (homeless for 2 1/2 years).

Sam Worthingtin . . . actor (car for a time while a struggling actor) (source: various, news interview: "I was living in my car before I signed up for 'Avatar'." / *Star* magazine, January 11, 2010, page 14: "Before *Avatar*, the actor admits, he was 'living in his car.'").

John Woo . . . Chinese-born film director (*Mission Impossible 2, Broken Arrow, Windtalkers,* etc.) (outdoor camping/crude shelter; homeless at age seven along with his family after a major fire in Hong Kong on Christmas Day 1953 destroyed his home and those of 50,000 other residents: "There was a big fire. We were homeless for a year. We lost everything.").

Charles Gayle . . . jazz musician (streets and abandoned buildings in New York City).

Debbie Reynolds . . . **Oscar-nominated** and **Emmy Award-winning** actress-singer; American author (car for awhile after her divorce in 1973 from Harry Karl, as mentioned in her autobiography).

Cary Grant . . . . **Oscar-winning** actor (streets of Southampton, England during a summer in his youth at the time of World War I) (source: book, *Cary Grant: A Biography*, by Marc Eliot, 2004, page 31: "Archie then volunteered for summer work as a messenger and gofer on the military docks, often sleeping in alleys at night if he didn't make enough money to rent a cot in a flophouse.").

Rubina Ali . . . actress (age 9, outdoor camping in Mumbai, India after municipal workers destroyed her family's makeshift home located in the slums) (source: news.yahoo.com/s/eonline/124888, "She's world famous . . . and now homeless. The family of Rubina Ali, the 9-year-old girl who portrayed the young Latika in the Oscar-winning *Slumdog Millionaire*, is trying to find shelter after authorities in Mumbai bulldozed their shanty house. This comes less than a week after the home of costar Azharuddin Mohammed Ismail, 10 (young Salim) was demolished.").

Burl Ives . . . **Oscar-winning** actor; **Grammy Award-winning** folk singer; American author (freight trains/outdoor camping; hitchhiked in the 1930s while in his early 20s across America, Canada, and Mexico).

George Orwell . . . British author (shelter).

Charles Sanders Peirce . . . Harvard University-educated genius scientist; mathemetician; logician; philospher; American author; first psychologist elected to the National Academy of Sciences. (homeless and destitute for a time later in life, relied on charity from friends).

Harry Edmund Martinson . . . Nobel Prize-winning Swedish author (abandoned by his mother at an early age along with his sisters when his father died; later as an adult, he traveled for a time on a "homeless tramp" as a vagrant and vagabond, experiences that provided the basis for some of his writings).

Don Imus . . . radio-show host; photographer; **best-selling American author** (between the dryers in a Laundromat in Hollywood, California).

John Muir . . . early American naturalist; advocate for the creation of U.S. national parks; founder of the Sierra Club; author (outdoor camping/farms/a cemetary; traveled by foot from Indianapolis, Indiana to the Gulf of Mexico coast in southern Florida).

Woody Guthrie . . . folk singer-songwriter; Rock and Roll Hall of Fame inductee; author (freight trains/outdoor camping).

Philip Emeagwali . . . supercomputer scientist; lecturer; one of the pioneers of the Internet (refugee camps and abandoned buildings with his family during his childhood in Nigeria/streets of Washington DC).

Ed Mitchell . . . former television reporter for ITN, BBC, CNBC, and media organizations (a bench next to a nightclub in Hove, Sussex). (sources: *The Guardian*, December 15, 2007; *The Mail on Sunday*, December 16, 2007 and December 23, 2007).

Mary Gauthier . . . singer-songwriter (streets during her teen years after running away from her alcoholic parents' home).

Chris Thomas King . . . **Grammy Award-winning** American Blues musician; actor (public parks in London, England).

Eartha Kitt . . . **Grammy Award-nominated** singer; **Emmy Award-nominated** actress; American author (apartment building rooftops in New York City).

William Smith . . . early British geologist; cartographer; created the world's first geologic map in 1815; given the title "The Father of English Geology" (homeless for ten years due to debts after publishing his large format map; later recognized as a genius and given a lifelong pension by King William IV).

Michael Winslow . . . actor; vocal effects impressionist (Venice Beach in California for a time after hitchhiking from Colorado).

Terri White . . . Broadway actress-singer (park bench for three months in 2008 in Manhattan, New York City after losing her apartment) (source: *People* magazine, November 23, 2009, pg 120, "Homeless to Broadway": "Last year Toni nominee Terri White was sleeping on a park bench. Now she's living a dream.").

Joe Gilliam Jr. . . . American football player; youth football camp operator; played in two winning Super Bowl games; *Sports Illustrated* magazine cover subject September 23, 1974 (streets/sleeping in a cardboard box under a bridge in Nashville, Tennessee).

Randy Johnson . . . American NFL football player (Bread of Life Mission homeless shelter in Punta Gorda, Florida, 1999) (source: *Charlotte Sun* newspaper, Florida, May 10 1999, republished September 26, 2009 after his death).

Rob Thomas . . . **Grammy Award-winning** singer-songwriter (park benches/beach; homeless for three years after turning 17).

Henry Lee Jost . . . lawyer; mayor of Kansas City, Missouri USA 1912-1916 (streets of New York City during his childhood; sent west on one of many "orphan trains").

Tommy Tallarico . . . video game composer; writer-producer; elected to a term (2005-2007) on the Board of Governors of the National Academy of Recording Arts & Sciences (Grammy Awards) (Huntington Beach/car, for awhile after moving to Los Angeles from Springfield, Massachusetts).

Trasey Lewis . . . granddaughter of producer-writer-*Star Trek* creator Gene Roddenberry (shelter in Las Vegas, Nevada).

Scott Stapp . . . **Grammy Award-winning** singer-songwriter; lead vocalist of the band "Creed" (car).

J.R. Richard (Janis Rodney Richard) . . . Houston Astros baseball player (under an Interstate highway bridge in Houston, Texas).

Dick Lane . . . American football player; National Football League Hall of Fame inductee (abandoned in a dumpster at the age of three months and then adopted by the woman who found him) (source: *Time* magazine, February 11, 2002, obituary).

Traci Lords . . . actress-singer-songwriter; American author; former model (outdoor camping while a youth under a bridge one night with other runaway youths, as described in her autobiography *Underneath It All*).

Darryl Rouson . . . Florida State Representative; lawyer; political activist (floor of an office building for a brief period, early 2000s) (source: *Miami Herald*, April 21, 2010: "Rep. Darryl Rouson, D-St. Petersburg, said he used to be homeless about a decade ago and slept on the floor of an office building. 'I understand homelessness,' he said. 'I understand what it means to wash off in a public bathroom. This bill [making homelessness a hate crime in Florida] seeks to protect our weakest.'"

Colin McCabe . . . Scottish-born actor (vacant building next to Union Train Station in Los Angeles).

Sam McClain . . . **Grammy Award-nominated** blues singer (streets of Pensacola, Florida).

Pat McDonough . . . American author; Pulitzer Prize nominee (homeless shelter in Minneapolis, Minnesota USA during the winter of 1983-1984).

Rose McGowan . . . actress (streets/sleeping in nightclubs in Portland, Oregon).

Frank O'Dea . . . (Francis O'Dea) Canadian author, businessman, humanitarian (steets of Toronto; shelter) (source: autobiography *When All You Have Is Hope*, 2007, by Frank O'Dea).

Michael Oher . . . American NFL football player; subject of the 2006 book *The Blind Side: Evolution of a Game* and 2009 film *The Blind Side* (nominated for Best Picture Oscar) starring Sandra Bullock (winner, Best Actress Oscar) and Quinton Aaron as Oher. (homeless for a time as a teenager in Memphis, Tennessee).

APPENDIX C
SOME TRUTHS FROM OTHER PEOPLE

CHILDREN LEARN WHAT THEY LIVE BY DOROTHY LAW NOLTE, PH.D.

If children live with criticism, they learn to condemn.

If children live with hostility, they learn to fight.

If children live with fear, they learn to be apprehensive.

If children live with pity, they learn to feel sorry for themselves.

If children live with ridicule, they learn to feel shy.

If children live with jealousy, they learn to feel envy.

If children live with shame, they learn to feel guilty.

If children live with encouragement, they learn confidence.

If children live with tolerance, they learn patience.

If children live with praise, they learn appreciation.

If children live with acceptance, they learn to love.

If children live with approval, they learn to like themselves.

If children live with recognition, they learn it is good to have a goal.

If children live with sharing, they learn generosity.

If children live with honesty, they learn truthfulness.

If children live with fairness, they learn justice.

If children live with kindness and consideration, they learn respect.

If children live with security, they learn to have faith in themselves and in those about them.

If children live with friendliness, they learn the world is a nice place in which to live.

LET IT GO!
BY BISHOP T.D. JAKES

There are people who can walk away from you. And hear me when I tell you this! When people can walk away from you—let them walk.

I don't want you to try to talk another person into staying with you, loving you, calling you, caring about you, coming to see you, staying attached to you. I mean hang up the phone.

When people can walk away from you let them walk. Your destiny is never tied to anybody that left. The bible said that, *"they came out from us that it might be made manifest that they were not for us; for had they been of us, no doubt they would have continued with us"* (1 John 2:19).

People leave you because they are not joined to you. And if they are not joined to you, you can't make them stay—let them go!

And it doesn't mean that they are a bad person. It just means that their part in the story is over. And you've got to know when people's part in your story is over so that you don't keep trying to raise the dead. You've got to know when it's dead. You've got to know when it's over.

Let me tell you something, I've got the gift of good-bye. It's the tenth spiritual gift. I believe in good-bye. It's not that I'm hateful, it's that I'm faithful, and I know whatever God means for me to have—He'll give it to me. And if it takes too much sweat, I don't need it.

Stop begging people to stay. Let them go!

If you are holding on to something that doesn't belong to you and was never intended for your life then you need to—let it go!

If you are holding on to past hurts and pains—let it go!

If someone can't treat you right, love you back, and see your worth—let it go!

If someone has angered you—let it go!

If you are holding on to some thoughts of evil and revenge—let it go!

If you are involved in a wrong relationship or addiction—let it go!

If you are holding on to a job that no longer meets your needs or talents—let it go!

If you have a bad attitude—let it go!

If you keep judging others to make yourself feel better—let it go!

If you're stuck in the past and God is trying to take you to a new level in Him—let it go!

If you are struggling with the healing of a broken relationship—let it go!

If you keep trying to help someone who won't even try to help themselves—let it go!

If you're feeling depressed and stressed—let it go!

If there is a particular situation that you are so used to handling yourself and God is saying "take your hands off of it," then you need to—let it go!

Let the past be the past. Forget the former things. God is doing a new thing for [you]!

Let it go!

ATTITUDE
BY CHARLES SWINDOLL

The longer I live, the more I realize the impact of attitude on life.

Attitude to me is more important than facts.

It is more important than the past,

Than education, than money,

Than circumstances, than failures, than successes,

Than what other people think or say or do.

It is more important than appearance, giftedness, or skill.

It will make or break a company.

It will cause a church to soar or sink.

It will be the difference in a happy home or a home of horror.

The remarkable thing is you have a choice every day regarding the attitude you will embrace for that day.

We cannot change our past.

We cannot change the fact that people will act a certain way.

We cannot change the inevitable.

The only thing we can do is play on the one string we have, and that is our attitude.

I am convinced that life is 10 percent what happens to me and 90 percent how I react to it.

And so it is with you.

APPENDIX D
AN EXAMPLE OF TRUE LOVE AND NORMAL PARENTING

Overcome Being Poor or Homeless

SUNDAY Daily News
dailynews.com

SUNDAY, MAY 13, 2007

Mom's pride

25 years after his bleak beginning, adopted crack baby earns law degree

Although doctors said D.D. Pawley would be mentally delayed because he was born addicted to crack, he persevered to graduate from law school on Friday, thanks to the love of his adoptive mom, Ila, and dad, Dale.

Parents' love proves ultimate cure

"After Dale and I had three children of our own, we decided we didn't need any more images of ourselves — not when there were so many other kids out there needing a home."

— Ila Pawley, mother of 11 adopted and three biological children

dennis McCARTHY

The kid came into this world with two strikes against him. Then he hit a home run.

Ila Pawley became his mom.

"I got lucky. So lucky," D.D. Pawley said Friday as he slipped on his cap and gown. "If it wasn't for her love and all the sacrifices she made for me, I wouldn't be standing here today."

A young man with a bright future, getting his law degree from the Sandra Day O'Connor College of Law at Arizona State University and starting his career in a few weeks as a deputy district attorney in Sacramento.

Not bad for a kid who came into this world 25 years ago as a drug-addicted, African-American baby found abandoned outside a Los Angeles hospital.

D.D. — Dale David — was 3 days old and weighed just 4 pounds when Los Angeles County adoption workers called the Pawleys and asked the middle-aged white couple living in Arleta if they had room for one more.

They had already adopted and raised three children of mixed races, in addition to three children of their own. But, sure, they had room for one more, Ila Pawley told the county.

This one would be the toughest, the doctors warned her.

PLEASE SEE **McCARTHY / PAGE 15**

Overcome Being Poor or Homeless

McCARTHY:
Family helps crack baby beat the odds

CONTINUED FROM PAGE 1

Because of the drugs in his system at birth, he would be slow. His motor-control skills would be poor, and he would be mentally delayed.

Pawley smiled and told the doctors to let her worry about that.

She had plans for this abandoned baby, and they all called for a lot of love and hard work.

That's what she told me back in 1998 when we stood watching her "slow" son, D.D., walk on stage to give the valedictorian speech at Osborne Christian School in Arleta as he graduated with a 3.97 grade-point average.

And that's what she told me again Friday as she watched D.D. put on his cap and gown and get ready to graduate from law school.

"Honest to God, I get chills," she said.

▫ ▫ ▫

Pawley won't forget those first nights looking down in the crib and seeing D.D. crying and squirming, curled up tightly in a fetal position.

Or the hours she massaged his body to relax his muscles and uncurl him.

Or the nights she and her husband, Dale, didn't sleep because D.D. didn't sleep.

"We'd hold D.D. all night, hold him on our chests so he could hear our heartbeats," she said.

"Nobody really knew diddly about drug-addicted babies back then. He should have been in the hospital during those withdrawals, but he wasn't.

"Dale and I read everything we could get our hands on and even went up to Stanford University to talk to doctors working with drug babies up there," Ila Pawley said.

"You know what turned out to work best? Normal parenting. Love, hugging, caring, teaching.

"We started him with words and listening to classical music. We showed him colors Legos, blocks, anything that would stimulate him. Everything but television.

"By the time D.D. started kindergarten, he could already read," she said. "He still had a sleep disorder and some motor-skill problems, but academically he was excelling."

Ila Pawley's plans for the most challenging child she would raise were working.

All it was taking was a lot of love and a ton of hard work.

▫ ▫ ▫

She can't even imagine life without this boy, Pawley said Friday, getting ready to go to the graduation ceremony with her husband and a couple of their older children who were able to get off work to travel to Arizona with them.

They all turned out great — all 11 children she and Dale adopted, and the three they had themselves in what Ila calls "the first batch."

"They've all stayed in touch with each other," she said. "The first batch loves the second batch. Everybody's doing fine."

The love this woman gave him, well, he's almost taken that for granted by now, D.D. said. He never lived a day under her roof when he didn't feel it.

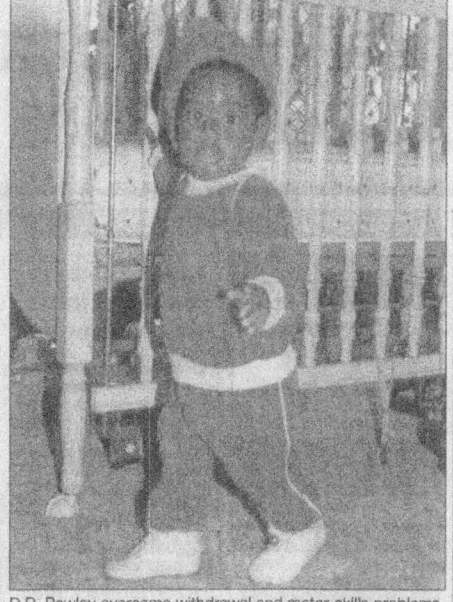

D.D. Pawley overcame withdrawal and motor-skills problems.

The hard work, though, that's what really gets to him now that he's married and a dad with two babies of his own.

"I think back on how tough it must have been for her to be raising all my brothers and sisters, and then have this sick little crack baby come into her life," D.D. said.

"She was willing to sacrifice so much for me.

"I know I've gotten my perseverance and resolve from her. She taught me you only lose if you quit and give up, and that's something I would never do.

"She's my rock, and I love her."

With that, the kid who came into this world a crack baby with two strikes against him gave his mother a hug and kiss before walking off to receive his degree from the Sandra Day O'Connor College of Law.

Leaving his mom standing there with tears in her eyes, and getting chills.

Dennis McCarthy's column appears Tuesday, Thursday, Friday and Sunday.
dennis.mccarthy@dailynews.com
(818) 713-3749

APPENDIX E
THE CHARITABLE-INDUSTRIAL COMPLEX

NoVo Foundation
create. Change

http://novofoundation.org/

The Charitable-Industrial Complex
27 July 2013
BY Peter Buffett

I had spent much of my life writing music for commercials, film and television and knew little about the world of philanthropy as practiced by the very wealthy until what I call the big bang happened in 2006. That year, my father, Warren Buffett, made good on his commitment to give nearly all of his accumulated wealth back to society. In addition to making several large donations, he added generously to the three foundations that my parents had created years earlier, one for each of their children to run.

Early on in our philanthropic journey, my wife and I became aware of something I started to call Philanthropic Colonialism. I noticed that a donor had the urge to "save the day" in some fashion. People (including me) who had very little knowledge of a particular place would think that they could solve a local problem. Whether it involved farming methods, education practices, job training or business development, over and over I would hear people discuss transplanting what worked in one setting directly into another with little regard for culture, geography or societal norms.

Often the results of our decisions had unintended consequences; distributing condoms to stop the spread of AIDS in a brothel area ended up creating a higher price for unprotected sex.

But now I think something even more damaging is going on.

Because of who my father is, I've been able to occupy some seats I never expected to sit in. Inside any important philanthropy meeting, you witness heads of state meeting with investment managers and corporate leaders. All are searching for answers with their right hand to problems that others in the room have created with their left. There are plenty of statistics that tell us that inequality is continually rising. At the same time, according to the Urban Institute, the nonprofit sector has been steadily growing. Between 2001 and 2011, the number of nonprofits increased 25 percent. Their growth rate now exceeds that of both the business and government sectors. It's a massive business, with approximately $316 billion given away in 2012 in the United States alone and more than 9.4 million employed.

Philanthropy has become the "it" vehicle to level the playing field and has generated a growing number of gatherings, workshops and affinity groups.

As more lives and communities are destroyed by the system that creates vast amounts of wealth for the few, the more heroic it sounds to "give back." It's what I would call "conscience laundering" — feeling better about accumulating more than any one person could possibly need to live on by sprinkling a little around as an act of charity.

But this just keeps the existing structure of inequality in place. The rich sleep better at night, while others get just enough to keep the pot from boiling over. Nearly every time someone feels better by doing good, on the other side of the world (or street), someone else is further locked into a system that will not allow the true flourishing of his or her nature or the opportunity to live a joyful and fulfilled life.

And with more business-minded folks getting into the act, business principles are trumpeted as an important element to add to the philanthropic sector. I now hear people ask, "what's the R.O.I.?" when it comes to alleviating human suffering, as if return on investment were the only measure of success. Micro-lending and financial literacy (now I'm going to upset people who are wonderful folks and a few dear friends) — what is this really about? People will certainly learn how to integrate into our system of debt and repayment with interest. People will rise above making $2 a day to enter our world of goods and services so they can buy more. But doesn't all this just feed the beast? I'm really not calling for an end to capitalism; I'm calling for humanism.

Often I hear people say, "if only they had what we have" (clean water, access to health products and free markets, better education, safer living conditions). Yes, these are all important. But no "charitable" (I hate that word) intervention can solve any of these issues. It can only kick the can down the road.

My wife and I know we don't have the answers, but we do know how to listen. As we learn, we will continue to support conditions for systemic change.

It's time for a new operating system. Not a 2.0 or a 3.0, but something built from the ground up. New code.

What we have is a crisis of imagination. Albert Einstein said that you cannot solve a problem with the same mind-set that created it. Foundation dollars should be the best "risk capital" out there.

There are people working hard at showing examples of other ways to live in a functioning society that truly creates greater prosperity for all (and I don't mean more people getting to have more stuff).

Money should be spent trying out concepts that shatter current structures and systems that have turned much of the world into one vast market. Is progress really Wi-Fi on every street corner? No. It's when no 13-year-old girl on the planet gets sold for sex. But as long as most folks are patting themselves on the back for charitable acts, we've got a perpetual poverty machine.

It's an old story; we really need a new one.

∞

Roland John Gilbert Biography

Mental illness and case management is the modern plantation for the poor and uneducated.

Roland Gilbert's father was born around 1900 and his grandfather was born prior to 1865 into legalized slavery in the southern United States. Roland's father could not read or write, yet he successfully learned to be a chef cook and protect and provide for his wife and 3 children until he died in 1978. "I am so proud of my grandfather and father because they had to overcome such tremendous obstacles to succeed. I am also proud of those 4 million Africans freed in 1865 after 246 years of being enslaved and then in less than 2 lifetimes (144 years) Barack Obama is President of the United States of America," says Roland.

Roland grew up poor in South Los Angeles, California and lived through President Lyndon B. Johnson's trillion dollar War on Poverty. Roland says, "People remain poor because they lack economic, social, cultural and symbolic capital and do not know how to avoid symbolic violence. I have invested 25 years of my life teaching the poor how to gain the capital they need and avoid being victims. My mission in life is teaching people how to discover and cultivate their greatness and give their gifts to the world."

Mr. Gilbert is the author of 3 books: ***The Ghetto Solution***, ***Power Parenting for Poor People***, and ***Overcome Being Poor or Homeless.*** He says he has, at least, 2 more books to write. Roland has now spent 25 years answering God's call to help poor people succeed. He founded the nationally acclaimed Simba Program in Oakland, California and was Executive Director for 15 years. Simba helped inner city youth and adults overcome self-destructive attitudes and behaviors and achieve more success in their lives. Mr. Gilbert's work is endorsed by many distinguished experts including Alvin F. Poussaint, M.D., Clinical Professor of Psychiatry, Harvard Medical School; James P. Comer, M.D., Maurice Falk Professor of Child Psychiatry, Yale School of Medicine; and Deborah Prothrow-Stith, M.D., Assistant Dean of Government and Community Programs, Harvard School of Public Health.

Currently, and throughout the last 6 years, he serves as the Professional Development Instructor for the Skid Row Development Corporation in Downtown Los Angeles, California and also provides consulting services through his company Power Parenting. He is proud to serve on the Los Angeles Regional Homeless Restoration Advisory Coalition Board of Directors.

Among his outstanding notables, President Jimmy Carter selected him for national program management and appointed Mr. Gilbert to the United States Small Business Administration, in Washington, D.C., as a Business Revitalization Specialist. Roland was instrumental in leveraging $100 million into $1 billion of financing for 26 cities within one year. Who's Who in Finance and Industry recognized Mr. Gilbert for his accomplishments.

Made in the USA
Coppell, TX
25 May 2023

17290360R00056